Original title:
Whispers Beneath the Christmas Tree

Copyright © 2024 Creative Arts Management OÜ
All rights reserved.

Author: Adrian Caldwell
ISBN HARDBACK: 978-9916-94-388-5
ISBN PAPERBACK: 978-9916-94-389-2

Gentle Voices of the Season

Giggles echo in the air,
As pinecones tumble down with flair.
A cat attempts to climb so high,
While stockings sway, oh my oh my!

The cookies call, a sweet delight,
But tummies rumble, what a sight!
The reindeer prance with jingle bells,
A dance-off starts with silly yells!

Side Notes of Snowy Nights

Snowflakes land on noses bright,
As cocoa spills in pure delight.
The snowman winks with a silly grin,
Oh, how hard it is to keep him thin!

Sledding down the hill, what fun,
A race erupts, but who has won?
The puppy hops, his tail a blur,
In all the chaos, a goat does stir!

Lullabies Amidst Twinkling Lights

Stars are twinkling, light so bright,
But Santa's lost his map tonight!
He checks his list, oh, what a mess,
Did he forget to wear his dress?

The elves are giggling, making toys,
While reindeer play with squeaky joys.
A mistletoe hangs, a chance to kiss,
But someone slips, and oh, what bliss!

Shadows of Laughter in the Stillness

Bubbles float in warm hot tubs,
As dad dons hats, quite the duds.
The fire crackles, tales are spun,
Of how grandma beat us in a run!

A game of charades begins to rise,
Dad mimics snowmen, oh what a surprise!
Sisters tackle, tickles galore,
Laughter bursts through the open door!

Embraces of Moments Past

In jolly socks with pudding stains,
The cat finds joy in gift-wrap chains.
Old photos laugh from dusty shelves,
While grandma's tales are told by elves.

We giggle at the wig on Dad,
That silly look makes everyone mad.
A dance-off starts, a clumsy show,
As Uncle Joe joins in the flow.

Threads of Warmth on a Frosty Eve

Hot cocoa spills, marshmallows dance,
My sister's laugh: a clumsy prance.
A snowman forms, all crooked and round,
He waves hello, but then falls down.

Grandpa's sweater, two sizes too wide,
With buttons popping on every side.
We cozy up near the flame's glow,
As shadows of laughter begin to grow.

Sighs of Happiness in Quiet Corners

Under the tree, a gift unwrapped,
It's socks for socks, my mind is zapped.
The cat, confused by all the cheer,
Decides the tinsel needs a leer.

A cookie thief, it's my little brother,
He's caught red-handed by our mother.
Chocolate smudges, a guilty grin,
He claims the cookie had a twin!

Interludes of Peace and Charity

Around the table, stories flow,
Auntie's hat falls off, oh what a show!
With laughter rising like the pie,
It's hard to breathe; we can't deny.

We share our woes, the mishaps told,
Of snowmen falling, a sight so bold.
A toast to joy, and all we miss,
And chocolate fudge, a savory bliss!

Heartbeats Wrapped in Greenery

In the hush of night so bright,
Tinsel fights with dogs in flight.
Ornaments swing, a chaotic dance,
Cousins giggle, not a chance!

Each bauble holds a secret cheer,
A cat in a crown, we all wear near.
A tree so tall, it seems to sway,
Must be the eggnog gone astray!

The Quiet Murmurs of Togetherness

Grandma's sweater, a sight to see,
Patterns of snowflakes, or was it a bee?
Uncles joke as the kids run wild,
Not one takes heed of the dog, oh mild!

Flashing lights blink like a disco ball,
While Auntie sings and we mock her call.
We gather close 'round snacks galore,
Is it really Christmas or just a food war?

Flickers of Light in the Depth of Night

Little hands reach for the glow,
Finding secrets they long to stow.
A gift too big, it tips and falls,
Wondering where it's coming from, the calls!

Socks unruly, tossed on the floor,
Who needs pajamas when toys outscore?
The clock ticks slow, but laughter flies,
As Santa's sleigh breaks down – oh, what a surprise!

Hidden Hues of Family Joy

In the corner lurks an elf on strike,
Stuck to the cat, oh, what a hike!
Sisters plot with giggles loud,
Christmas stories turned upside down!

Cookies burn, a festive break,
Who knew laughter could make a cake?
With each mishap, the love expands,
Creating chaos, together we stand!

Echoes of Solace in the December Chill

Socks hanging low, they might just fall,
A cat in the tinsel, oh look at it sprawl.
The tree's grown a beard, with stray needles in tow,
Grandma's got cookies, but who needs 'em? No show!

Rudolph's red nose is bright like a flare,
But where's all the candy? It vanished in air.
The lights keep on flickering like they're in a race,
Who needs a gym when you've got this place?

Elves making mischief, oh what a sight,
Spilled all the cocoa, the floor's a new fright.
The garland's a jungle, it sways to the beat,
Dance with the ornaments, stomp your own feet!

Mittens are mismatched, they laugh with glee,
Reindeer games grinning, as silly as can be.
The joy of the season, with giggles and cheer,
Echoes of solace, let's spread it all year!

Shadows of Kindness Under Crystalline Lights

Ghosts of old cookies dance on the floor,
Great-aunt Edna brought fruitcake; we shut the door.
Snowflakes are falling, just like in a dream,
But the kids are outside, plotting their scheme.

The lights on the tree are tangled like yarn,
Someone just dropped a gift—oh no, it's a darn!
Gnomes tucked in corners, with mischief to spare,
All plotting together to ruin our hair.

Santa's been spotted, or was it a cat?
Funny how holiday moments grow fat.
The stockings are stuffed, overflowing with treats,
But first, someone's hiding our favorite sweets!

In shadows of kindness, laughter will swell,
With gifts wrapped in giggles, unspoken as well.
Crisp winter mornings and snowball fights bright,
Celebrate love, 'neath these crystalline lights!

An Embrace of Seasons Past

Nostalgic the hugs from ornaments old,
Each telling a story, laughter retold.
The wreath on the door, a bit crooked in place,
And Uncle Bob's sweater—what a wild space!

Frosty's a legend, but look at him melt,
He shivers and shakes, but oh how he felt.
Carols are sung with a wink and a grin,
Who says holiday cheer can't be joined by spin?

Traditions are tangled like strings in a ball,
Mom's fruitcake is ready; oh, do take a hall!
The echo of laughter, it rings through each home,
A dance with the past, through all we have known.

Moments are fleeting, yet cherished so tight,
Embrace all the seasons, both day and night.
The sparkle of joy radiates through this cast,
In every sweet memory, an embrace of the past!

Radiant Graces Hidden in Stillness

Under the blankets, the stockings hide cheer,
Piggy banks jingle—a sound that we hear.
The glitter and glimmer delight at first sight,
But where's all the good stuff? Check under the light!

Hot cocoa is steaming, but wait, what's the fuss?
A marshmallow snowman was just squished by us.
The cookies, half-eaten, call for some more,
This merriment's balancing on one tilted floor.

Pine needles scatter like confetti on ground,
The dog steals a present, oh what have we found?
Each giggle and chuckle wrapped up oh so tight,
Radiant graces are hidden in night.

Laughter erupts, in the glow of the room,
Even the cat's wrapped up tight in the gloom.
Beneath all the chaos, this season we treasure,
Finding pure joy is the ultimate measure!

Solstice Songs Beneath Spruce and Fir

The cat's upon the lights, oh dear,
Spinning round like a little sphere.
Grandma's cookies vanished quick,
Was it the elf or Uncle Rick?

Snowflakes dance with a funny buzz,
While kids stick noses to the fuzz.
A penguin in a Santa cap,
Leaves no room for a quiet nap.

The tree is leaning to one side,
Caught in a tinsel-tangled ride.
Socks now hang, mismatched and keen,
What happened to our golden sheen?

Laughter bounces off the walls,
As the dog decides to take some falls.
In this chaos, joy takes lead,
Underneath, that's all we need.

Reflections of Love in Icy Mirrors

Frosty windows hide the scene,
Someone's wearing a jolly green.
With mismatched socks, we laugh and cheer,
While puffing out that Christmas beer.

The mistletoe's a cheeky thief,
Stealing kisses from disbelief.
A snowman wobbles, arms outstretched,
Too much fun, he's quite the sketch!

Grandpa's stories twist and twirl,
As Grandma's knitting starts to swirl.
Yarn balls roll, we chase in glee,
These frosty days, oh what a spree!

As we toast to holiday quirks,
The silliness truly works.
In every chuckle, love does thrive,
Togetherness, we feel so alive!

The Unseen Glow of Togetherness

Underneath the blinking cheer,
Someone slipped, spilled hot root beer.
Unexpected giggles split the air,
Who knew winter holds such flair?

Baked goods fight for space on plates,
While dances spark some funny states.
A bear in a scarf? Oh, what a sight,
Turns every evening into delight!

The clock strikes one, and chaos reigns,
As snowflakes flutter down like chains.
Siblings wrestling on the floor,
Joyful shouts echo more and more.

In every corner, laughter hides,
As Santa's hat on the dog abides.
A holiday mix of love and fun,
Unseen glow; we've just begun!

Fantasies Adrift on December Breezes

In December's chill, we make a scene,
Laughing at dreams, silly and green.
Candy canes play tag with the air,
While reindeer fly without a care.

The cocoa's steaming, oh so sweet,
But watch out now or you'll lose your seat!
As uncle shares tales, the cat sneezes wide,
A heaping bowl of laughter inside.

Twinkling lights in a tangle fight,
As dad declares he's the Christmas knight.
A card game breaks into friendly war,
With goofy jokes that leave us sore.

As the night wraps us up in fun,
The echoes of joy have just begun.
In these crazy moments, we all decree,
Together is the best place to be!

Tender Hearts Nestled in Evergreen

Tiny elves try to sneak,
With cookies and milk, they peek.
Tinsel tangled in their hair,
They giggle, causing quite the scare.

Cats batting at the baubles,
Caught red-pawed with no troubles.
Under the starry glow they scheme,
Planning more mischief than one can dream.

A snowman falling on his face,
In all the fluff, he finds his place.
Hot cocoa spills, but laughter flows,
As merry chaos expertly grows.

With candy canes strung like lights,
Jingle bells clash in silly fights.
Beneath the boughs of bright surprise,
The holiday spirit never lies.

Memories Adorned with Winter's Touch

A turkey dance takes center stage,
As Grandma's jokes turn every page.
Uncles trip over their own feet,
While kids take cover, it's quite a feat.

Wrapping paper flies like snow,
What's in the box? We want to know!
A gift for you, a sock for me,
The laughter rings, a joyful spree.

If Frosty's carrot starts to melt,
Who will confess the chaos felt?
Hidden gifts and silly tunes,
Echoing in the afternoon.

Roasting chestnuts with some flair,
Dad's dance moves spark the air.
We cherish these quirks, all in jest,
In winter's grasp, we are all blessed.

A Symphony of Twilight Awaits

The cat pounces on the lights,
Sparks and giggles, playful sights.
Magical creatures jump about,
No idea what this fuss is about!

Grandpa snoozes in the chair,
Dreaming of presents everywhere.
While children plot, with eyes aglow,
A secret mission, oh, let it flow!

Snowflakes fall on frosty ground,
As toys march forth without a sound.
In the dance of dusk, they play,
A zany twist to holiday sway.

Dinner's ready, come delight,
With grumbling tummies, it's quite the sight.
Bursting laughter, turkey and glee,
The fun escalates, just wait and see!

Delicate Whispers of Holiday Tales

The tree lights flicker, what a scene,
A mischievous mouse might just be seen.
He swipes a cookie on the run,
Squeaking tales of holiday fun.

Socks on the dog, what a sight,
He prances proudly left and right.
Wrapped up tight in colorful bows,
Chewing on something, how it goes!

Pine scent mingles with tinsel bright,
Footsteps dancing in the night.
Uncle Fred tells stories old,
While a snowball fight starts to unfold.

Laughter ring as we unwrap,
Finding more than a single gap.
With jolly spirits and good cheer,
We treasure these tales year after year.

Unveiling Glimmers of Nostalgia

Tangled lights, a festive sight,
Grandma's cookies, a pure delight.
Cousins giggle, stories intertwine,
Gift-wrapped jokes, oh how they shine!

The cat climbs high, it takes a fall,
A tree of tinsel, we deck the hall.
Mom's in charge, with a roll of tape,
While Dad's stuck in a reindeer cape!

Remember the time we lost the gifts?
Found in the attic, among odd bits.
Santa's hat on the dog so proud,
A memory of laughter, loud and loud!

With every sigh as the day ends,
We navigate this fam'ly blend.
As lights flicker, our smiles arise,
In these moments, laughter never dies.

The Essence of Togetherness Enfolded

In the kitchen, a dance of cheer,
Flour in hair, but who can care?
Dad's strange recipe, a curious pie,
Potatoes flying, oh my, oh my!

The dog in a sweater, what a sight,
Chewing on tinsel, what a fright.
Cousins squabble, a playful fight,
Over the last cookie, oh what a night!

Cards are read with exaggerated flair,
'The best of luck!' and 'Did you wear that hair?'
Laughter echoes from wall to wall,
Our goofy traditions, the best of all.

As the fire crackles, we start to fade,
From turkey to pudding, a happy cascade.
Snuggled tight, beneath the light,
In this chaos, everything feels right.

Nighttime Reveries Under Starry Skies

Under the stars, we share our dreams,
Mixing hot cocoa in wacky schemes.
S'mores gone awry, stuck in the fire,
Yet laughter blossoms, taking us higher.

A game of charades goes wildly wrong,
Imitating penguins, we sing a song.
From snowball fights to sliding on ice,
These holiday moments, oh how they entice!

Grandpa's tales, embellished and grand,
Of jellybeans and a grumpy old band.
As shadows dance under moonlit glow,
Each absurd story helps our hearts grow.

With the night deepening, we gather 'round,
Exchanging our secrets, no need for a sound.
As giggles and grins fill the chilly air,
In simple togetherness, we find our share.

Lullabies of the Frost-Kissed Night

Frosty flakes dance with glee,
A squirrel stole my cup of tea.
The lights flicker like fireflies,
While giggles echo, oh what a surprise!

Cookies hidden up so high,
Santa's diet? Oh, that's a lie!
Reindeer prance in jolly cheer,
While I chase them—oh dear, oh dear!

Under blankets, cats conspire,
They plot to knock down that new wire.
Presents tremble in their heap,
While I hope for just one sweet leap.

So gather 'round, let laughter roar,
Tickle the toes of the yule log floor.
With every giggle and beaming grin,
We mend our hearts, let the fun begin!

Notes of Nostalgia Amongst the Gifts

Beneath the bows, the secrets lie,
Mom's fruitcake? I might just cry!
An apron wrapped for Dad's big roast,
But really, it's just a buttered toast!

Cards scribbled with love, so grown,
From kids who stole my favorite bone.
A teapot pairs with socks so bright,
Why is the reindeer on a fright?

The dog barks to join in the fun,
As we trip over toys, oh what a run!
With every chuckle and every cheer,
We celebrate joy that draws us near.

So here's a toast with gingerbread toast,
To silly things we cherish most.
With laughter echoing, we'll reminisce,
For it's the quirky joys we can't miss!

The Unfolding of Winter's Embrace

Snowmen wobble with carrot noses,
While penguins dance in funny poses.
Flavored hot cocoa spills in delight,
As we catch marshmallows that take flight!

Frostbite nibbles at fingers and toes,
Yet laughter warms us as the chill grows.
With sleds that crash and giggles explode,
We race down hills like a super-code!

Taste of candy canes in the air,
As snowflakes land in a frosty stare.
Laughter echoes, children in glee,
Crafting a holiday jubilee!

For every mistletoe, we sneak a kiss,
While the cat hunts for sweet mistletoe bliss.
From holiday chaos, let laughter flee,
For this winter's heart, wild and free!

Silent Stories Wrapped in Ribbon

Presents tangled, bows askew,
What's in there? A sock or two?
The cat sits plotting her grand attack,
While I hope no one wears a Santa hat!

Beneath the tree, the tales unfold,
Of kids getting caught in the cold.
The night brings laughter, lights so bright,
And dreams of mischief dance in sight.

Grandpa speaks of days gone by,
With a twinkle, and oh, my, my!
The things he did—a tale so wild,
Makes me think of my inner child.

So unwrap the joy, with giggles galore,
For these are the gifts that we adore.
As stories linger on this night,
Let our hearts revel in holiday light!

Unseen Gifts of the Winter Solstice

Tiny elves twist and dance,
Bags of giggles in each glance.
Forgotten socks upon the floor,
Real gifts hide behind the door.

Tinsel tangled in a ball,
Santa's cap, it starts to fall.
Cookies vanished, crumbs afloat,
Oven burns, another note!

Ribbons tangled in a mess,
Who designed this holiday stress?
Gifts wrapped up with silly strings,
Laughter's what this season brings.

Surprises wait, oh what a sight,
Chasing shadows through the night.
Unseen laughter shines so bright,
Winter's magic takes its flight.

Echoes of Cheer in Candlelight

Candles flicker, wax does drip,
A cat jumps up, prepares to slip.
Mistletoe hangs a bit askew,
Dancing squirrels, just a few!

Giggling voices fill the air,
Clumsy friends forget to share.
Eggnog spills upon the floor,
Laughter echoes, 'Who wants more?'

Jingle bells, but someone's flat,
Reindeer waltz with a plump cat.
Holly leaves, they start to sing,
Joyful chaos is the fling.

With every flicker, stories told,
Of Santa's sneezes, brave and bold.
Echoes linger, sweet delight,
In the glow of candlelight.

Murmured Tales of Frost and Fire

Frosty noses peek and stare,
Fireplace crackles with a flare.
Sock puppets join the show,
Telling tales of winter's glow.

A snowman wears a silly hat,
Boxes spill—oh, where's the cat?
Hot cocoa spills, marshmallows flee,
Toasting toes, oh glee to see!

Gifts of laughter, tangled cheer,
Ghosts of Christmas past draw near.
Muffin tops, they start to roll,
As sugar plums dance in the bowl.

Silly stories, all around,
Echo hilarity, joy is found.
Frost and fire, hand in hand,
Murmuring fun across the land.

Hidden Wishes Amongst the Ornaments

Glistening baubles, hope they hide,
Pine needles scatter, a joyful ride.
Toys that giggle, ornaments sway,
What secrets bloom this holiday?

A gingerbread man plots his roam,
Candy canes search for a home.
Wrap the cat in shining bows,
Witness the holiday chaos grows!

A reindeer on a wild spree,
Chasing lights and giggling free.
Mismatched socks hang by design,
But hidden wishes still align.

With every jingle, laughter sings,
Among the trinkets, joy it brings.
Hidden wishes, cheerously blend,
In this season, laughter's a friend.

Secrets Wrapped in Frosted Tinsel

Beneath the sparkly cheer,

A cat plots to cause a fright.
With a leap and a bound,
Oh, what a curious sight!

The dog, with a bone in tow,
Schemes to take off with the loot.
While kids giggle in a row,
As they dodge the little brute!

Tinsel drapes like shiny hair,
On the dog with a happy face.
As the little ones shriek and stare,
Chaos is this festive place!

Maybe next year they'll behave,
Or perhaps cause more of a mess.
Until then, we'll just misbehave,
For laughter's the best Christmas dress!

Tides of Joy Under Glistening Boughs

A present sits too snug and tight,
What wonders lie inside?
Is it socks or is it fright?
The cat knows, with feline pride.

Children peek with sticky hands,
Right where the treats are stored.
Their plans to sneak make merry bands,
Of giggles they can't afford!

The tree shakes as they bounce about,
Or maybe it's just the cat.
Who knows what they're laughing about,
With bows tied on the mat!

Here's to holiday delight,
And children who cannot be tamed.
In the glow of twinkling light,
Every one of us feels the same!

Soft Hums of Yuletide Blessings

The stockings droop, they cannot hold,
The treats the kids have spied.
A chocolate thief, oh, bold!
Now let the Christmas fun abide!

With Santa's gift, the dog does prance,
Hiding behind the wobbly tree.
He steals a topper, what a chance!
And smiles, his secret just for me.

Children plotting, hearts will race,
Naughty lists are just a game.
Finding snacks in every space,
They'll never quite feel the same.

Around the fire, we all will sing,
To memories caught in the time.
In every laugh, the joy will cling,
This merry season's sweet rhyme!

Underneath the Evergreen Magic

Under the boughs where toys reside,
A giggle peeks from under the bag.
The secret's safe, they try to hide,
While the cat plans to have a brag.

A trail of glitter leads the way,
To cookies stashed for Santa's night.
But crumbs are scattered, oh what a play!
What mischief lies in that sweet bite?

Tiny hands unwrap with glee,
Voices rise in joyful cheer.
Each peek reveals a mystery,
And magic fills the atmosphere!

With every laugh under soft light,
The spirit grows, it's clear to see.
This holiday, pure and bright,
Forever wrapped in jokes and glee!

Subtle Revelations in the Glow

A squirrel found the stash of treats,
Underneath where Rudolph sleeps.
He giggled as he took a snack,
A holiday he won't take back.

The lights blink twice, a sneaky show,
Is it magic or just the snow?
Elves are plotting with no disguise,
As mischief twinkles in their eyes.

In the corner, a dog on guard,
Protecting gifts that are kind of charred.
With a bark and a playful leap,
He dreams of toys, not counting sheep.

So gather 'round, let stories flow,
Of holiday quirks and winter's glow.
Each laugh a gift that we unwrap,
In sweet embraces, there's no mishap.

Frosted Secrets and Swaying Pines

Underneath the branches wide,
A cat got tangled—what a ride!
With ornaments hanging from her tail,
She prances back like a little whale.

The star up top has lost its light,
It looks around, it's not quite bright.
Said the garland with a jolly twist,
"Let's party hard, you won't be missed!"

A mouse with courage bold and stout,
Wanders through, ready to scout.
He sings a tune of festive cheer,
While nibbling crumbs—oh dear, oh dear!

So dance beneath the leafy crowns,
As laughter skips and joy abounds.
For hidden tales in chimes we find,
All in good fun, with hearts entwined.

Threads of Love in Winter's Embrace

With mittens missing, we search in vain,
The snowman laughs as he feels no pain.
A carrot nose and swishing broom,
He sways along, brightening the gloom.

Mom pranced in with cookies galore,
But forgot the flour—what's an encore?
With sprinkles flying and cheers in tow,
She made a mess, but stole the show!

Three ghosts appear, in search of cheer,
But they forgot why they came here!
Instead, they danced to a jolly tune,
Under the watch of the silver moon.

In this season of tangled laughs,
We find the joy in silly gaffs.
So gather close, let friendships mend,
As we stitch our hearts, with laughter to blend.

Humble Stories of Silent Nights

In the attic, old toys hold a court,
Where teddy bears and dolls consort.
They gather round and spin their tales,
Of holiday feasts and snowy gales.

The gingerbread men begin to fight,
Over icing and candy, what a sight!
One trips on gumdrops, a tasty plight,
They laugh and tumble with all their might.

With candles lit, the shadows dance,
While cookies wink as if by chance.
"Won't you come join our silly spree?"
They giggle loud, just wait and see!

So let's toast to moments sweet and small,
In the glow of night, we cherish all.
For laughter's the gift that never decays,
While stories of silliness light our days.

Echoing Hopes in December's Chill

In the frost the squirrels play,
Tinsel tangles lead the way,
Snowmen dance with carrot noses,
While frozen hands grab Christmas poses.

Candy canes hang on the eaves,
Laughter spills like autumn leaves,
Gifts of socks and ties await,
As we ponder who's our fate.

Chubby cheer from Santa's sack,
Wrapped surprises all off track,
Socks and mittens in a heap,
Dreams that make our giggles leap.

Feline pounces at the glow,
Rolling in the gifts below,
Sprinkled joy in every line,
Even grumpy Uncle Mike.

Fragrant Memories Among the Limbs

Cinnamon swirls fill the air,
Baking cookies, laughter shares,
Mama's secrets, sprinkles bold,
Recipes passed down like gold.

Elves in aprons make a dash,
Cake pops tumble, what a crash!
Giggles echo through the hall,
As frosting flies and sprinkles fall.

Naughty pets steal shiny treats,
Wrapped surprises make for feats,
Grandma shouts, "Oh what a mess!",
As we grin in our Christmas dress.

Socks that wriggle on the floor,
Left by feet who ran for more,
Chaos reigns in joyful glee,
As we celebrate with tea.

Softly Stitched by Threads of Gold

Stockings stretch with silly shapes,
Filled with snacks and tubby grapes,
Laughter bubbles as we peek,
At who might be playing sneak.

DIY gifts with wobbly seams,
Knitted chaos, crafty dreams,
Pine scent solid in the air,
While paper fights provoke despair.

Lights that twinkle like our eyes,
Spilling secrets and surprise,
Fluffy slippers on our feet,
While we watch a holiday treat.

With every stitch and every cheer,
Mom declares "Let's drink some beer!"
We toast to silly, toast to fun,
In December's glow, we've just begun.

Luminous Dreams of Nighttime Revelry

Stars like cookies in the sky,
While reindeer prance, oh me, oh my!
The night is bright with youthful glee,
As carolers sing off-key with me.

Presents stacked in towers high,
Who will be first to spy?
Dad gets stuck beneath the tree,
A comedy for all to see!

Twinkling lights don't help a bit,
As cats attempt a daring split,
They chase the ornaments with fright,
Creating chaos late at night.

Merriment fills every nook,
As new traditions take a look,
We laugh and cheer, the morning breaks,
In tales we craft, our heart awakes.

Soft Serenades of the Holiday Hearth

The stockings are drooping, a sight most absurd,
My cat's plotting mischief, it's clearly inferred.
The cookies are missing, crumbs everywhere,
Mom's caught on video, dancing without care.

Lights blinking wildly, like stars gone astray,
Uncle Joe's snoring, in the midst of his play.
The tree leans to one side, with a grin extra wide,
It's wearing a star hat, refusing to hide.

Eggnog is flowing, with laughter galore,
Dad's telling tales of the Christmas before.
A reindeer is stuck on the roof, what a scene!
Our festive uproar is the best you have seen.

So gather around for the jolly old cheer,
With humor and joy, bring everyone near.
For laughter is the treasure, wrapped up with delight,
In the warmth of togetherness, everything feels right.

Echoes in the Candlelight

Flickering candles cast shadows that prance,
As Aunt Betty's dog tries to join in the dance.
She claims it's a gift, but we all know the truth,
That dog just wants treats, and he's stealthy forsooth.

The chimes ring a tune, on the hour they sound,
But Grandma's old phone, it just can't be found.
Cousins roll laughter like cookies on plates,
As Dad's inappropriate jokes ravage the fates.

The garland's a mess, with tinsel askew,
The tree's getting sappy, with glue weberoo.
The cat is now purring, all wrapped in the lights,
Chasing furballs of joy in the long winter nights.

So here's to the fun, let the echo resound,
For the magic of laughter is always around.
We'll cherish the chaos, every little part,
As the glow of the candles warms up every heart.

The Hidden Language of Festive Cheer

My brother is juggling the ornaments high,
As they crash to the ground, I can't help but cry.
But laughter erupts like a pop at the seams,
With glittery chaos replacing our dreams.

A snowman's been built, but it missed the big hat,
It's wearing a bucket, with a stare like a cat.
Mom's in the kitchen, wielding her spoon,
"Just add more sprinkles!" she'll sing like a tune.

The elf on the shelf is checking his phone,
Texting his buddies, "I'm never alone!"
The gifts are all wrapped, but one's upside down,
It's labeled for Grandma and meant for the clown.

So gather together, let laughter take flight,
As we cherish these moments, filled with delight.
The secrets we share, in our joyful embrace,
Are the gifts that keep giving, in life's merry race.

Secrets in the Grasp of Evergreens

In the corner, a pile of presents so grand,
But it's just Dad's old sweater, that's all he had planned.
Sister's new puppy is tangled in bows,
While the popcorn string melts in the warm glow.

Dad's trying to fix the lights on the tree,
But all that he's done is create more debris.
Mom's giggling softly, while observing the plight,
As our efforts to decorate have turned into fright.

The green garlands flutter, like dancing in glee,
While Cousin Lou acts like he's surfing the sea.
The ornaments wobble, each time we poke,
And Uncle Fred's laughing, he's choking on smoke.

So let's toast to the fun, with cocoa or cheer,
As we tuck in the memories we hold so dear.
Though secrets are hidden among branches, you see,
It's the laughter and love that's the best gift of glee.

Glimmers of Joy in the Dim Light

In the corner, shadows creep,
A cat's tail twitches, oh so deep.
Tinsel flies, a playful chase,
Santa's hat lost in the race.

Cookies crumble, crumbs in a trail,
The dog looks guilty, cannot say 'nail'.
Laughter echoes, glass filled with cheer,
While Uncle Joe sings, woefully unclear.

Lights flicker, a dance like a dream,
A candle leans, its wick starts to scream.
Mittens fly, a snowball fight,
As laughter melts the chilly night.

In this chaos, our hearts align,
Amidst the mischief, we find the divine.
One last cookie, we jest and tease,
With joy wrapped up as tight as a freeze.

Tender Stories Beneath Nature's Blanket

Snowflakes twirl on a sock puppet,
While Dad spills cider, what's the next setup?
Grandma's knitting, a tangled spree,
A blanket destined to fit a flea.

Fireside tales of battles won,
With toy soldiers, the victor's fun.
A squirrel peeks, outrageous and sly,
Stealing nuts like it's pie in the sky.

Twinkle lights strangle the tree,
A glowing wonder, as bright as can be.
Pudding spills, oh what a sight,
While laughter floats into the night.

In this moment, we bumble and bop,
We toast to the chaos, holding the crop.
Love and humor make for grand delight,
As stories unfurl under stars shining bright.

Glistening Silence of Gathered Hearts

Presents pile high, a pyramid scheme,
While laughter bursts, it feels like a dream.
A partridge squawks, a curious sound,
As aunties gossip, the secrets abound.

Laughter tickles, like snowflakes on skin,
Grandpa dances, a mishap begins.
Mistletoe's ready, a kiss gone wrong,
Oh, holiday antics where we all belong.

Chocolates melt in knowledgeable hands,
As kids conspire with sneaky plans.
The sprigs of pine, the scent so sweet,
While we chuckle over the last tasty treat.

Mom's eyeing the icing, oh what a battle,
With frosting galore, it's a sweetened saddle.
In our gathered hearts, a mischievous flair,
For in every chuckle, love fills the air.

Reveries in the Hushed Evening

A sock on the shelf, shoots for the moon,
While elves serenade us a timeless tune.
Leftover snacks pile up on the floor,
A hovercraft moment — oh, what's in store?

Snowmen jiggle, their buttons on fleek,
As we swap stories, cheek to cheek.
Grandpa snorts, takes a sip of cheer,
A tale as old as the holiday year.

Kittens frolic in wrapping delight,
They thwart our plans, oh what a sight!
With twinkling lights in the palms of our hands,
The night relies on our made-up strands.

As eyelids droop, we weave the fun,
In dreams of sugar, we become one.
Each chuckle shared, a gift to maintain,
In this gentle hush, we dance in the rain.

Melodies of the Year's Close

Jingle bells ringing, cats chasing the mice,
Leftover fruitcake, not so very nice.
Pine needles dropping, oh what a sight,
Fumbles on carpets, our friends take flight.

Hot cocoa spills as we cheer with a grin,
A scarf-ing competition, let the fun begin!
Laughter erupts with each awkward dance,
As grandma yells, 'What happened to my pants?'

Tinsel gets tangled; oh what a mess,
Each ornament tells tales of past excess.
With each clumsy step, we yell, "Take a seat!"
As cousins trip over their own two feet.

The clock strikes twelve, we all shout, "Hooray!"
But the fruitcake still lingers, it's here to stay.
Embracing the chaos, we raise our cheer,
Here's to the laughter of another bright year!

Beneath the Canopy of Hope

Lights strung up crooked, a festive delight,
A squirrel steals cookies to munch through the night.
Snowballs are flying, oh what a scene,
A snowman with sunglasses, quite a routine!

Grandpa's new sweater, a sight to behold,
It's red and it's green, and three sizes too bold.
The cat jumps and pounces, on the gifts piled high,
As we watch in sheer panic, and laugh 'til we cry.

The stockings are bulging, with odd little things,
A rubber chicken? What joy that brings!
We gather and giggle, the stories we share,
With hiccups and snorts, there's love in the air.

So here's to the quirks, the laughter and glee,
Each silly mishap, a part of our spree.
Beneath all the chaos, let joy take its flight,
For we're all together, and that feels just right!

Silent Wishes on Snowflakes' Wings

Snowflakes are drifting, like dreams from afar,
A penguin in pajamas, his own little star.
The cookies go missing, who could it be?
A sneaky old raccoon, as spry as can be.

The carolers sing, with their hats on askew,
While the families gather, for a raucous review.
Mismatched socks flutter, each child's delight,
As uncles attempt twirls, oh what a sight!

The candy canes vanish, just like our will,
A game of hot potato is starting to thrill.
With giggles and jabs, the mayhem unfolds,
As laughter's the treasure that never grows old.

So toast to the moments, both silly and sweet,
With cheers and with chuckles, we dance to the beat.
Silent wishes soar, on wings of delight,
With laughter as magic, we're lost in the night!

Echoing Hearts in Radiant Silence

In the hush of the eve, with a basket of cheer,
Grandma's secret eggnog, perhaps just a beer?
Puppies on leashes, trying to chase,
A tumble of pillows and giggles we face.

The fruitcake is mighty, a weapon of war,
"Take a big slice!" yells little Timmy, "More!"
As we plow through the dishes, the laughter runs free,
Echoing joy like a sweet melody.

The games that we played make us family strong,
From charades to card games, we can't go wrong.
As stories unfold and old jokes get retold,
Every chuckle and grin forms a bond to behold.

So here's to the moments, both funny and strange,
In the glow of the lights, may we never change.
Echoing hearts join together in glee,
In the fabulous chaos, we're happy and free!

Whispered Wishes in the Frost

In the corner, a cat takes a leap,
Chasing shadows, not a peep.
The lights twinkle, a sneaky game,
As if the tree is calling her name.

Cookies vanish, a plate left bare,
Santa's on a sugar high, beware!
The reindeer giggle, trying to land,
While elves are plotting, a prank so grand.

Tinsel tangled in dog's bright tail,
The puppy's proud—he thinks it's a sail.
Christmas cheer wrapped in ribbons wide,
But don't trust that grin, it's mischief that's tied.

Underneath those evergreen beams,
Dreams of gift-opening, candy, and screams.
Laughter echoes, stories ignite,
As we dance 'round in pure delight.

The Silent Chorus of Evergreen

A squirrel sneaks in, oh what a sight,
Nibbling ornaments, late in the night.
The garland sways with a little jig,
As laughter erupts from a tiny twig.

All the toys come alive with glee,
Huddled in whispers, under the tree.
The teddy bear offers a secret sip,
With a wink and a nudge, let joy slip.

Jingle bells clash, a comical ring,
As the notes dance like butterflies in spring.
An elf on a shelf does a backflip too,
Scaring the cat, who knew not what to do.

Gifts of socks, and bright candy canes,
Wrapped in laughter where silliness reigns.
The stars above chuckle and twirl,
As holiday cheer makes the world swirl.

Tales from the Twinkling Ornaments

Once a bauble rolled far from the floor,
Singing carols with matching decor.
It tripped on a present, fell with a clatter,
Creating a scene that didn't quite matter.

Jolly old St. Nick dropped his snack,
A cookie avalanche, oh what a stack!
The reindeer giggle at the sight of it,
While Santa debates where to sit and split.

An icicle glints, sharing a joke,
With a gift-wrapped banana, to smoke or not smoke?
The mischief unfolds beneath shiny bows,
As the laughter of the ornaments grows.

With winks exchanged and a wink from a pine,
The stories unravel as though they align.
The tree shakes with joy, lights flicker bright,
In this funny place where magic takes flight.

Unseen Stories of Winter's Eve

From the basement, a rumble of fun,
As the lights come alive, a race has begun.
The snowman outside is plotting a scheme,
To scare kids away, oh, it's quite the dream!

A pickle ornament hides on the ledge,
Challenging fortunes—a game, it can hedge.
The cat in the corner, tail in a twist,
Fails to catch it, too caught in the mist.

Sprinkles of snow from the roof above,
Land on the tree in a wintry shove.
Little elves giggle, spreading delight,
Creating a scene that's a pure, silly sight.

While mittens toast by a crackling fire,
The memories gather, never to tire.
With chuckles and cheer, the night feels aglow,
In this merry mishap, let laughter flow.

The Glow of Unspoken Traditions

The lights blink in rhythm, oh what a scene,
A cat on the table, it thinks it's a queen.
The cookies are missing, the milk's gone too,
Who ate all the snacks? Was it me or you?

Grandma's old sweater, a sight to behold,
It fits like a sack, but it never gets old.
We laugh through the stories, and roll up our eyes,
As uncles regale us with previous lies.

The fruitcake is sitting, all hard as a rock,
We offer a slice to our neighbor named Brock.
He nibbles and winks, then he starts to choke,
"I swear this is safer than it looks," he joked!

The gifts are all wrapped with questionable care,
To find what's inside? Who knows, if we dare.
Yet laughter and chaos, they fill up the room,
With each silly mishap, we banish the gloom.

Soft Breaths in the Chilly Air

In the yard, Santa's sleigh hides from view,
Along with his reindeer who ate all the stew.
The snowman is leaning, he's got a small grin,
Did someone teach him how to spin?

Mittens mismatched, all tangled and frayed,
Once comfy and warm, now a cold serenade.
The snowball fight starts, oh what a delight,
But someone gets hit—was that Aunt Sue's fright?

We hang our old socks on the mantle with flair,
Will they fill with small treasures or just some despair?
An orange or coal? It's a thrilling toss-up,
Can we flip to decide? Or just keep it up?

The carols we're singing are silly at best,
With lyrics all jumbled, we laugh with the rest.
Yet fondness surrounds us, we smile through it all,
It's fun, and tradition—when family's the call.

Mysteries of the Longest Night

Lights twinkle above, like stars on the floor,
But one bulb is blinking, what's happening for sure?
The cat's plotting mischief, perched high in the tree,
As we ponder the mysteries that hide, oh so free.

Uncle Joe is snoring, a sound like a train,
We wonder how long 'til he wakes up again.
The clock strikes the hour, the cookies are gone,
Did the elves take the last bite, or just our own spawn?

The stories get taller with every round told,
About Grandma's great mishap—it never gets old.
While shadows invade, a prank's in the air,
Who'll find the long gift that's hidden somewhere?

We dance with the chaos, in jolly delight,
Knowing tomorrow will be a fun-filled sight.
For family and laughter, in this sacred space,
We cherish each moment, and everyone's face.

Softly Spoken Sentiments

The ornaments shimmer, each one tells a tale,
Of when Auntie fell down while trying to sail.
The popcorn's been strung, yet the dog claims the prize,
He munches and crunches, right under our eyes.

The stockings line up, each one full of cheer,
Does anyone notice Grandpa's quiet beer?
He chuckles and smiles, with a glint in his eye,
As we swap silly jokes, how time does fly!

The sound of the laughter, it fills up the room,
A mixed bag of memories that started to bloom.
And as stories unwind, they twirl 'round the night,
In this rowdy reunion, everything feels right.

With each goofy gesture and heartfelt embrace,
These moments of warmth we can never replace.
So let's raise a cheer, for the fun and the glee,
In this merry old gathering, just you, and me!

Voices of the Silent Night

In the stillness, a giggle grows,
Beneath the sky that sparkles and glows.
Santa's sleigh gets stuck in the snow,
Reindeer muffle, as the laughter flows.

A gift unwraps, and what do we see?
A sock filled with jellybeans, oh me!
With jingles and jangles, the fun starts anew,
Hiding the pickles for the whole crew!

Cookies are missing from the plate by the fire,
Elves blame the cat, who will never tire.
A dance in the moonlight, just look at them prance,
Under twinkling stars, they join in the glance.

Laughter erupts from the depths of the frost,
'Tis the season for mischief, no matter the cost.
As snowflakes tumble and tickle the cheek,
The night is ablaze with the joy we seek.

Messages from the Forest Floor

Amidst the pines, a squirrel takes heed,
While tripping on acorns, he finds quite the speed.
Beneath the holly, a raccoon's parade,
Stealing the snacks that the kids had made.

Mice hold a conference, discussing their cheese,
While under the branches, they feast with such ease.
A paper hat, made from wrapping so bright,
Transforms the old dog into king for the night!

Frosty the snowman starts to complain,
His carrot nose feels the winter's disdain.
"Why can't we party?" he shouts with delight,
As snowballs fly, creating a sight!

An owl on a branch takes notes, quite astute,
While giggling at antics in the furry suit.
Nature applauds, this silly ballet,
As the forest joins in on the festive display.

Flickering Hints of a Snowy Tale

In the barren yard where the snowflakes land,
A snowman worries, there's work to be planned.
His hat's made of fruitcake, not quite what he likes,
While birds throw confetti from nests on their bikes.

The chimney puffs out a cloud of sweet scent,
While reindeer in training make quite the event.
"Higher!", they shout, as one fails to leap,
Tales of their blunders are bound to be cheap.

Mittens are lost during snowball fights,
Impulsive exchanges inspire pure delights.
The dog wears a scarf, quite stylish and neat,
Yet trips on a snowdrift and lands at their feet!

By the bonfire, the family comes near,
Held up by a snowman who can't share his beer.
So they chuckle and tease this chilly old chap,
With frosty drinks in this festive mishap!

Beneath the Boughs of Celebration

Beneath the branches, a party ensues,
With jingling laughter and holiday blues.
A cat in a tinsel, with glittery flair,
Declares to the world, "I'm the star, beware!"

Gifts wrapped in laughter and volume galore,
Are opened with glee that shakes the floor.
"Is this a toaster? I wanted a bike!"
As Grandma's new gadget ignites with a spark.

A parrot is singing, off-key yet bold,
Tales of Christmas from stories of old.
"Deck the halls with holly, but where's my snack?"
While someone stumbles on the holiday rack.

Outside the window, a snowman looks in,
As the party erupts, let the nonsense begin!
A night full of chuckles, a season so bright,
Together we celebrate 'til morning's first light.

Enigmas of the Season's Light

Tiny lights twinkle bright,
Chasing shadows in the night.
Elves are giggling, what a sight,
Searching for cookies, what a bite!

Frosty noses, scarves in tow,
Sledding down the hill we go.
Snowballs fly, oh what a show,
Laughter echoes, spirits glow.

Mystery gifts piled so high,
Who wrapped this? Oh my, oh my!
A cat in a box, I can't deny,
Reindeer games make time fly.

Under boughs, secrets laid,
Old toys found, memories replayed.
Jokes of Santa, and how he played,
With every moment, cheer won't fade.

Hidden Treasures of Christmas Past

Grandma's cookies, oh what bliss,
Who would think they taste like this?
Percy the turtle gives a hiss,
As Auntie sings her off-key kiss.

An old snow globe, cracked and worn,
Reminds us of the years reborn.
In the attic, treasures adorn,
Christmas cheer through giggles sworn.

Mismatched stockings hang with grace,
Each with a story, a silly face.
Unwrapping laughter at a slow pace,
Finding fun in every space.

Under the bed, a prank unfolds,
Plastic bugs and treasure troves.
Who knew the laughter that it molds?
Hidden gems, our heart engulfs.

Silent Echoes of Letting Go

The tree's shedding needles now,
Santa's beard is losing brow.
Rudolph's nose just won't allow,
To shine again, oh dear, oh how!

Toys are tired, their battery's low,
A wooden train that used to go.
In silence, old stories flow,
Letting go, but spreading glow.

Frosty's hat sits lonely, still,
While kids race on, their hearts to fill.
Yet every laugh and every thrill,
Lives on inside, they can't kill.

Through bittersweet, we jovially glide,
Holding onto joy, our hearts are wide.
In letting go, love's not denied,
Memories dance, our faithful guide.

The Untold Chronicles of Winter Wonder

While snowflakes fall, stories take flight,
A penguin slides left, then right.
Talking trees share secret delight,
With giggles that echo through the night.

Hot cocoa spills, the puppy sneezes,
In winter's chill, laughter pleases.
Invisible elves with painted cheeses,
Wreaking havoc, as joy increases.

Under the glimmer, truths unfold,
In the chaos, warmth takes hold.
Mishaps and laughter, new and old,
Our hearts aglow, worth more than gold.

With every tale, let us explore,
The magic that we all adore.
In winter's grip, we laugh some more,
Adventures boundless, life's a score.

Embracing the Stillness of Celebration

In the corner, tinsel sparkles bright,
A cat leaps high, a comical sight.
Cookies crumble in a clumsy mess,
As Auntie trips, it's quite the fest!

Beneath the branches, gifts piled high,
Grandpa snores, we dare not pry.
A prancing elf with mismatched shoes,
Belly shakes with each laugh, we can't refuse!

Mistletoe hangs, but who will chance,
A smooch with Cousin Ed—oh, what a dance!
The joy is loud, the smiles aglow,
In this chaos, love tends to grow.

So gather 'round, let the stories unfold,
In our hearts, these memories are gold.
With laughter shared, we'll raise a toast,
To the quirks of family we love the most.

An Ode to Moments Wrapped in Time

The clock ticks slow, the cocoa brews,
Balloons float high—wait, those aren't ours!
A gift unwrapped, surprise galore,
It's a rubber chicken, who could ask for more?

Upon the table, a feast awaits,
But watch for the dog and his sneaky traits!
He's plotting, planning, wiggling his tail,
As Grandma warns, her effort won't fail.

A photo snapped, laughter ignites,
Uncle Joe's face—a sight that delights!
Mismatched socks and hats gone awry,
Time stands still as we crack up and sigh.

So raise a glass to these moments we make,
In the silly, sweet chaos, joy's no mistake!
Each chuckle and grin, a treasure to find,
In time's tender embrace, we all unwind.

Secrets Carried on the Wind

Outside it rumbles, a storm passing by,
Yet here in the warmth, not a single sigh.
A cousin confesses with a mischievous grin,
I borrowed your gift, but it's time to begin!

Laughter erupts as stories are told,
From years long gone, feeling brave, feeling bold.
The cat, with attitude, claims the best chair,
While we squeeze in tight, as if we could care!

Under the lights, the chaos anew,
A forgotten mixtape, from '92?
The tunes spin tales of our wild youth,
While we dance like pros (or so we think—truth!)

So here's to the secrets we've buried so deep,
And moments we've shared that now make us peep!
With hearts all aglow, and spirits that sing,
We'll cherish these times that each holiday brings.

Traces of Laughter in Still Waters

A splash in the bowl, the punch overflows,
As little ones grin, while Granny just dozes.
They fling confetti, a glittery sight,
And giggles erupt, filling up the night!

The snowflakes dance in the chilly air,
While Uncle Bob's tales take us somewhere.
With each silly gesture, he captures the crowd,
As we all lean in, laughter erupts loud!

A game of charades—oh, what a delight,
As Dad turns into a lobster, it's quite the sight!
Each gesture exaggerated, each line a mistake,
No one can breathe, oh what a break!

So let kindness twinkle, let laughter abound,
In the heart of the season, love can be found.
These moments, now treasured, will help us remember,
The joy that we share in this silly December!

Murmurs of Joy from the Hearth

The stockings are hung, all in a row,
With candy canes bursting, oh what a show!
Uncle Joe's snoring, his face in the pie,
A chorus of laughter, and oh my, oh my!

The cat on the table thinks it's a feast,
He swipes at the cookies, from greatest to least.
With tinsel and giggles, we dance in our socks,
While dodging the dog that is dressed like a fox!

The candles are flickering, lights all aglow,
As Grandma tells tales that are starting to grow.
A sweater so hideous, Dad wears with pride,
It jingles and jingles while we try to hide!

With eggnog in hand, we toast to the night,
As Auntie's wild fruitcake takes off in flight.
The joy of the season, all wrapped up in cheer,
Murmurs of laughter, we hold so dear!

Reverberations of Goodwill in the Air.

The tree is a beacon, it's bigger than life,
With baubles and garlands, it sparks joy and strife.
Cousin Tim's prank with the strings of the lights,
Ends up in chaos, oh what funny sights!

Grandpa's new gadget goes beep, beep, beep,
While under the table, the dog is asleep.
But wait, who just shouted? Oh no, it's a flop!
The moment he leans, the presents all drop!

With candy-filled stockings, and jokes in the air,
We gather around, family love everywhere.
Mirthful exchanges, we giggle and tease,
As Mom shouts, "Not my fruitcake, please!"

The laughter resounds like a festive parade,
In this jolly mess, memories are made.
Reverberations ringing out loud and clear,
In this joyful chaos, we hold so dear!

Silent Echoes of Holiday Dreams

The fireplace crackles, with sparks that do dance,
As mistletoe hangs, a curious chance.
Two kids in the corner, plotting a scheme,
To sneak out for cookies, like characters in a dream.

A reindeer plush snickers, its eyes in a glare,
It knows of the secrets we'd rather not share.
With giggles like whispers, we plan our misdeeds,
While Santa's sleigh swoops in to fulfill our needs!

Beneath all the wrapping, we find a surprise,
A gift wrapped so tight, even we can't surmise.
With bows and ribbons that dance in the light,
The suspense gets our giggles to hit such a height!

The echoes of laughter, they bounce off the walls,
In this blissful madness, the spirit enthralls.
Silent night's joys, wrapped tight in each beam,
In our holiday bubble, we giggle and dream!

Murmurs in the Heart of Winter

Snowflakes drift softly, like feathers in flight,
While cousins all gather, it feels just right.
The snowman stands solemn, adorned with a hat,
Yet giggles erupt when we see him go splat!

With cocoa in hand and marshmallows afloat,
We toast to the mishaps and cheer for the goat.
Uncle Bob stumbles, his dance moves a sight,
As we burst into laughter, it's pure delight!

The tree may be lopsided, but that's just our flair,
With baubles that dangle from here to nowhere.
We gather together, our spirits so bright,
Murmurs of warmth, in this cold winter night!

As we hum holiday tunes with a jolly old spin,
We cherish each moment, let the fun begin!
In the heart of the winter, with giggles in tow,
The season of joy sets our laughter aglow!

Secrets Among the Pine Needles

The cat is perched where gifts reside,
Tangled bows, a playful slide.
A sneaky elf with mischief at hand,
Hiding presents across the land.

A squirrel snickers from his spot,
He knows what's wrapped, he knows a lot.
The cookies baked, yet somehow gone,
Santa's reindeer laugh, 'Come on!'

Each ornament holds giggles tight,
As children peek in pure delight.
The lights blink twice, a secret beat,
Can't wait for the big feast to meet!

In the branches, stories crawl,
Of how the stockings tried to brawl.
The tree stands tall, so green and bright,
Underneath, the fun takes flight!

Echoes of Yuletide Dreams

The reindeer play a game of tag,
While visions dance around the snag.
Mistletoe hangs, but who's that brave?
A cheeky kiss? It's yet to save!

A snowman fumbles, hat askew,
His carrot nose? A booger too!
Giggling kids with lots to say,
How did this holiday go astray?

In the glow, the lights go dim,
As grandma hums a quirky hymn.
The stockings wiggle, filled with cheer,
Who knows what's lurking in here?

Beneath the stars, a secret swirls,
About Santa's strange antics, unfurls.
With laughter shared in festive gleam,
These echoes weave a funny dream!

Murmurs in the Holiday Glow

A cookie jar with missing treats,
There's crumbs where filched delight repeats.
A grin from dad, what's he to fear?
Did he eat Santa's snacks, oh dear?

The lights are strung, yet one is dead,
A frown on mom, a shaking head.
"Who broke the chain?" she playfully scolds,
While laughter erupts, old tales retold.

Tinsel flies, and cats take flight,
Knocking down baubles, oh what a sight!
Naughty tales of festive cheer,
Collected giggles fill the atmosphere.

The laughter fades, the night draws near,
With every sparkle, joy is clear.
And though the chaos may take its toll,
These murmurings fill the heart and soul!

Shadows Wrapped in Tinsel

A shadow slides beneath the pine,
Swiping gifts, now that's just fine.
Who knew that dad would steal the show,
While kids chase him laughing in a row?

The cookies gone, what a surprise,
Mom's glaring eyes, mischief flies.
Underneath the shiny wrap,
A space for pranks in every gap!

An ornament glimmers, whispers call,
"Time for a dance! Come one and all!"
The tree shakes as families prance,
With silly moves, they take a chance!

As laughter echoes, midnight nears,
Mischief reigns, yet love perseveres.
In shadows wrapped, the fun won't cease,
These moments capture joy and peace!

The Soft Sigh of Holiday Spirit

Tinsel tangled in the cat,
As she lounges, oh so fat.
Gifts stacked high with bows so bright,
Ribbons gone, what a funny sight.

Grandma's cookies in a jar,
Screaming 'Eat me!' from afar.
But one bite and oh dear me,
Sugar rush and chaos spree.

Stockings hanging with care,
Filled with socks and some despair.
Santa's list, a great big mess,
He must like to play, I guess.

Under the lights, we all sing,
Chasing cats, what joy they bring.
Joy and jingle, let's all cheer,
For holiday mishaps, warm and near.

Unspoken Bonds Under the Glow

Twinkling lights on every bough,
Napping pets, just don't ask how.
Hot cocoa spills on my new shirt,
I swear I'm more careful, don't assert.

Socks from grandma, one left here,
Chasing after it, oh dear!
Lost my thoughts under the cheer,
Cousins laughing, who's gonna steer?

Ornaments that dance and sway,
Echo memories of yesterday.
Grandpa's stories, all retold,
Each one funnier as they unfold.

Tangled tales and goofy grins,
Family wins and silly sins.
With every cheer and little tease,
We gather 'round like fallen leaves.

Memories Hiding in the Pine's Heart

The tree is dressed, but wait a sec,
What's that bulge? A plumber's wreck?
Gifts took a ride, oh what a fright,
One's a cactus, a true delight.

Baking cookies, what a sight,
Flour flying, it's a fight!
Gingerbread men dance away,
Too quick for us, what can we say?

Counting ornaments, who's the best?
Who forgot to clean the nest?
Birds are chirping, joining fun,
They may just snack on cookies run!

Holiday sweaters, oh so loud,
Fuzzy patterns, stand out proud.
With every giggle, joy we find,
Laughter's magic entwined, unconfined.

Flickers of Magic in December's Breath

Lights flicker, what a scene,
Caught my eye, was that a bean?
Silly string upon the floor,
Look, it's stretching through the door!

Snowmen built with oddest hats,
With mismatched gloves from petting cats.
They melt away, but what a dream,
Next year, we'll add whipped cream!

Family photos, smiles so wide,
In a frenzy, we all collide.
Caught a glimpse of Uncle Greg,
His dance moves, oh, they make me beg!

Joy and jests, they fill the air,
Santa's hat on my brother's hair.
With every grin, the warmth we keep,
In this funny, merry heap.

Milton Keynes UK
Ingram Content Group UK Ltd.
UKHW021939121124
451129UK00007B/145

9 789916 943885